Dinosaurs and Prehistoric Animals

Brachiosaurus

by Carol K. Lindeen

Consulting Editor: Gail Saunders-Smith, PhD

Consultant: Jack Horner, Curator of Paleontology
Museum of the Rockies
Bozeman, Montana

Capstone
press
Mankato, Minnesota

Pebble Plus is published by Capstone Press,
151 Good Counsel Drive, P.O. Box 669, Mankato, Minnesota 56002.
www.capstonepress.com

1 2 3 4 5 6 10 09 08 07 06 05

Library of Congress Cataloging-in-Publication Data
Lindeen, Carol K., 1976–
    Brachiosaurus / by Carol K. Lindeen.
    p. cm.—(Pebble plus. Dinosaurs and prehistoric animals)
    Includes bibliographical references and index.
    Summary: "Simple text and illustrations present the life of brachiosaurus, how it looked,
and its behavior"—Provided by publisher.
    ISBN 0-7368-4257-8 (hardcover)
    1. Brachiosaurus—Juvenile literature. I. Title. II. Series.
QE862.S3L494 2006
567.913—dc22   2004026742

Editorial Credits
Sarah L. Schuette, editor; Linda Clavel, set designer; Bobbi J. Dey, book designer; Wanda Winch, photo researcher

Illustration and Photo Credits
Jon Hughes, illustrator
© The Field Museum, #GN86878_11c/John Weinstein, 21

Note to Parents and Teachers

The Dinosaurs and Prehistoric Animals set supports national science standards related
to the evolution of life. This book describes and illustrates brachiosaurus. The images
support early readers in understanding the text. The repetition of words and phrases
helps early readers learn new words. This book also introduces early readers to
subject-specific vocabulary words, which are defined in the Glossary section. Early
readers may need assistance to read some words and to use the Table of Contents,
Glossary, Read More, Internet Sites, and Index sections of the book.

Table of Contents

A Huge Dinosaur

Brachiosaurus was a very tall
and heavy dinosaur.
It was one of
the biggest dinosaurs
to ever live on Earth.

Brachiosaurus lived
in prehistoric times.
It lived about 160 million
years ago in North America,
Europe, and Africa.

How Brachiosaurus Looked

Brachiosaurus was as tall

as a four-story building.

It was about 45 feet

(14 meters) tall.

9

Brachiosaurus walked
on four strong legs.
It had claws on its feet.

Brachiosaurus had nostrils

on its forehead.

It used its nostrils

to smell.

Brachiosaurus had
a very long neck.
It could reach high treetops.

What Brachiosaurus Did

Brachiosaurus ate ferns

and other plants

all day long.

It needed a lot of food

because it was so big.

Brachiosaurus moved
in herds.
Adults kept the young
safe from predators.

The End of Brachiosaurus

The last brachiosaurus died

about 145 million years ago.

No one knows why

they all died.

You can see brachiosaurus

fossils in museums.

Glossary

dinosaur—a large reptile that lived on land in prehistoric times

fossil—the remains or traces of an animal or a plant, preserved as rock

herd—a large group of animals

museum—a place where objects of art, history, or science are shown

nostril—an opening of an animal's nose through which it breathes and smells

predator—an animal that hunts other animals for food

prehistoric—very, very old; prehistoric means belonging to a time before history was written down.

Read More

Cohen, Daniel. *Brachiosaurus.* Discovering Dinosaurs. Mankato, Minn.: Bridgestone Books, 2003.

Goecke, Michael P. *Brachiosaurus.* Dinosaurs. A Buddy Book. Edina, Minn.: Abdo, 2002.

Matthews, Rupert. *Brachiosaurus.* Gone Forever! Chicago: Heinemann, 2003.

Internet Sites

FactHound offers a safe, fun way to find Internet sites related to this book. All of the sites on FactHound have been researched by our staff.

Here's how:

1. Visit *www.facthound.com*

2. Type in this special code **0736842578** for age-appropriate sites. Or enter a search word related to this book for a more general search.

3. Click on the **Fetch It** button.

FactHound will fetch the best sites for you!

Index

Word Count: 143
Grade: 1
Early-Intervention Level: 16